# THE

# FAITH-FILLED

# CLASSROOM

## top 10 ideas that really work

# THE
# FAITH-FILLED
# CLASSROOM

## top 10 ideas
## that really work

*Anne Campbell*
*Kathy Hendricks*
*Jacquie Jambor*
*Eileen McGrath*
*Kate Ristow*

**RCL**

Allen, Texas

Send all inquiries to:
Resources for Christian Living
200 East Bethany Drive
Allen, Texas 75002-3804

Telephone: 877-275-4725
Fax:        800-688-8356

E-mail: cservice@rcl-enterprises.com
Visit us at www.rclweb.com

Printed in the United States of America

**21115**    ISBN 0-7829-1062-9

7  8  9  10  11  12  13
06  07  08  09  10  11

# Contents

# INTRODUCTION

This book is written for parents, teachers, volunteers, and all those who are involved in the religious formation of children. You are all vital links between students and their faith development. You enable them to learn about their Church's teaching and to know how very much they are loved by God.

Parents, you are the child's first teacher and role model, the one who instills lessons of faith and morals in your children. Your faith, example, and lived reality set the stage and plant the seeds that become the groundwork for your child's religious growth. You play a major role between your child and the life of the parish.

Teachers and volunteers, you become the nurturers and coworkers as you continue, by your teaching and example, to "water the seeds" planted by parents. You are a valuable "natural resource" as you encourage children and youth to deepen their relationship with God, their families, their friends, and their faith communities. It takes a concentrated effort, all of you, working together to enhance the religious formation of children.

This book is an accumulation of ideas, thoughts, and techniques, put together by professional teachers and religious educators with a combined total of well over 100 years' experience. Hopefully, these tried-and-true suggestions can be used by all of you to make your sharing of faith and knowledge a little easier and make your interaction with the "religious life" of children more effective and even fun. Using these handy tips may enable you to make religion come alive and be more meaningful for the children. They are written succinctly, to be readily used by new or experienced parents, teachers, and volunteers. Some ideas may be very new to you and others may be familiar, because they work and have been "steady-enders" over the years.

Teachers have been taught to plan their work and work their plan. Whether you are in a formal classroom situation or sharing your faith at home, a well-orchestrated religion lesson with some extra activities for backup and other creative ideas can enhance the process of religious learning for your children.

There are other books on the market dedicated to very specific topics such as ways to teach religion, the use of discipline at home or in school, and classroom activities. This book contains an abundance of varied ideas in one place for your convenience and easy use. We know your life is full, and the quality time you have with your children or students can slip by quickly. Some ideas recorded here can be used specifically in a classroom setting, while others may be shared at home with the family. We hope this book will not only be placed on your bookshelf, but will also be a constant companion and easy resource as you prepare to teach a class or wish to make religion a more meaningful experience, as you encourage children to grow in their faith and their relationship with their God, family, friends, and community.

# −1−

# *SACRAMENTS, SEASONS, AND SCRIPTURE*

The religious formation of children is really a lifelong process. We said in the introduction that this journey begins in the home and continues through your example and through formal classes and teaching of religion. We also know from Scripture that there is a time, a season for everything. There are certain milestones, age-appropriate times when children are able to comprehend certain teachings of their religion. Times when they become "fuller participants," active members in their Church. Times when they develop a deeper, more diverse appreciation of prayer and the sacraments. There are teachable moments in their daily lives when children can spontaneously learn a truth of their religion. Chapter 1 shares some ideas and ways to enhance and share these special moments and ceremonies in the life of the children and their families.

## 10 Ideas for Making First Eucharist More Meaningful

1. Collect bread recipes from families in the program and compile a cookbook. Children can decorate the covers and give these to their parents as a reminder of the profound symbolism of bread.

2. Show the children (and families) the "Be Our Guest" sequence from the movie *Beauty and the Beast* (Walt Disney.) Talk about the joy and welcome of this meal for Belle, and link it to the joy and welcome that Jesus gives us through the gift of the Eucharist.

3. Discuss the differing expectations that a family has for children when they move from the high chair to the table. Link this to the differing expectations that now accompany their movement to receiving the Eucharist with the rest of the community. As they move to the Table of the Lord, what expectations does the Church have of them now?

4. Familiarize the children with the different symbols and gestures of the Mass. Over several weeks, take one or two symbols, prayers, or gestures and go over these with them. Helping children participate more fully in the liturgy is one of the most valuable parts of First Eucharist preparation.

5. Plan a classroom or family feast, comprised of favorite foods. Take a group poll and pick out 5 or 6 foods that everyone likes. Enlist the help of parents and other volunteers to prepare the food. Think about other touches that will make this feast special—table decorations, music, a special place to eat, and so on.

6. Have the children interview someone in their family—a parent, grandparent, older sibling, aunt, or uncle—about their memories of First Eucharist. Have them share one or two highlights of that interview with the rest of the class.

7. Help the children become familiar with the many gospel stories that are linked with the Eucharist, such as the Last Supper, the feeding of the five thousand, the wedding feast at Cana, the disciples on the road to Emmaus. Have them pick a favorite story and draw a picture illustrating it.

8. Write a letter to parents or guardians asking them to share the memories of their child's baptism with their child. This could include taking out photos and

baptismal garments, candle, and other mementos of that time. If the baptismal date is not known, invite the parents/guardians to share memories of the child's first birthday.

9. Make a class time line listing birthdays and baptismal dates. Cap the end of the time line with the scheduled date of First Communion. Allow the children the chance to decorate it as they wish.

10. Arrange for a tour of the church by contacting the pastor or director of religious education. Ask someone to lead the students through the different sections of the church—vestibule, sanctuary, and sacristy, for example, and to explain the different symbols and objects used for worship.

## 10 Ideas for Making First Reconciliation More Meaningful

1. Have the children act out some of the forgiveness stories in the Gospels—the prodigal son, the woman at the well, the woman being stoned, the forgiving servant—to name a few.

2. Watch the video clip from *Home Alone,* where Kevin visits the church and meets his elderly neighbor. Have the children discuss who "confesses" in the scene, who is forgiven, how Kevin and his neighbor become reconciled, and what they give one another before Kevin leaves the church.

3. Show Jiminy Crickett's song, "Always Let Your Conscience Be Your Guide," from Walt Disney's *Pinocchio*. Let the children use this as a way to discuss what a conscience is. Ask them to write their own "examination of conscience"—a way to help them remember what they need to do to stay faithful to God's love and teaching.

4. For older children, make a collage of magazine and newspaper pictures and stories that depict "social sin." These might depict war, violence, environmental destruction, or racism as a way of illustrating sin that is perpetrated by and harms the entire global community.

5. Brainstorm together ways in which peace is destroyed and how it can be restored—in families, schools, local neighborhoods, and the world. Help students see how they can be a force for peace by being aware of these things and acting to rectify them.

6. Visit the Reconciliation Room in the church. If possible, ask the pastor or director of religious education to guide the class into the room and explain its different symbols. Take time to say a prayer in the church before departing.

7. Give each student a copy of the Prayer of St. Francis. Have them memorize it or illustrate it.

8. Make up conflict scenarios and ask the children to find ways to resolve them. A scenario might show, for example, a fight between two siblings over watching the television, or an argument on the playground about sharing a ball. Make special note of any good conflict-resolution techniques that are named.

9. Create poster art depicting what a forgiving family (or parish or school or neighborhood, and so on.) looks like. What characterizes such a group? Encourage creativity!

10. Look up and read together gospel parables on forgiveness, such as the lost sheep (Luke 15:3–7), the lost coin (Luke 15:8–10), or the prodigal son (Luke 15:11–32). Act these out or have the children create cartoon panels to illustrate them.

## 10 Ideas for Making Confirmation More Meaningful

1. Establish prayer "angels" for each student. This could be either a sponsor, a member of the parish community, or a student from another parish or school.

2. Arrange for student pen pals. This might be someone who has been confirmed or is preparing to be, or someone who lives in another parish, town, or country.

3. Invite a guest to class who will speak on the gifts of the Holy Spirit or another topic pertinent to the students.

4. Have the children research the name they will take and share its meaning and the gifts of the person bearing the name.

5. Study the gifts of the Holy Spirit—wisdom, understanding, counsel, fortitude, knowledge, piety, and fear of the Lord. Ask the children to write about how they can use each gift in their daily life.

6. Put on a mock trial. Ask the students to demonstrate how one could be "convicted" of being a Christian because of their lifestyle and behavior.

7. Have the children investigate the different areas of ministry taking place within the parish. They can research parish bulletins and newsletters, and interview committee and staff members. Pull together the results of all of their work in a summary of parish ministry. Then invite each student to write or speak about an area of ministry which most impressed them.

8. Likewise, engage the students in a research project based on the variety of ministries taking place throughout the diocese. Invite a member of the diocesan staff to come and address the class.

9. If the students are involved in service projects as a part of their confirmation preparation, compile a listing of the different ways that this is being carried out and keep this updated as the date of the Confirmation ritual approaches.

1 0. Ask the pastor or director of religious education for a list of names of the catechumens and candidates preparing for the initiation sacraments. Include these names in your class prayers, reminding the students of the other members of the community who are also preparing to enter more fully into active participation within the Church.

## 10 Ways to Celebrate Advent

1. Have a St. Nicholas Day celebration on or near December 6. Provide candy canes for each student and explain the link between the shape of the candy and a bishop's crosier. Offer a prayer of blessing over the candy canes before distributing. Make a class or family Christmas card for your local bishop and send it to him.

2. Advent is a time of expectation and hope. Invite an expectant mother and/or father to class to talk about their hopes and dreams at this time in their lives. Include all expectant families in your class Advent prayers throughout the season.

3. The great feasts of the Immaculate Conception (December 8) and Our Lady of Guadalupe (December 12) occur during Advent. Have a Madonna fest by bringing to class different types of art depicting the Blessed Mother. Ask the parents of your students to bring in any statues or pictures they have to share.

4. If your class/family uses an Advent wreath, have the children compose prayers for the lighting of each of the four candles.

5. Arrange for a visit from John the Baptist or another character from the Christmas story. Ask a parent, friend, member of the parish youth group, or anyone else with a flair for the dramatic to dress up and pay a surprise visit to the class. During that time the character can explain his or her relationship to Jesus and allow the class to ask questions.

6. Create a class/family wish list—what the children would like Jesus to bring to their families, their towns, the world. Have each of the children create a paper star and write their wishes on them. Suspend the stars from the ceiling or hang them on a Christmas tree or bulletin board.

7. Share Christmas memories. Ask the children to write or draw their warmest memory of Christmas. Have them bring this home to a parent or family member as a way to express their appreciation for this blessed time of year.

8. Read aloud the Christmas canticles of Mary (Luke 1:46–55) and Zechariah (Luke 1:67–79.) Provide copies for the students and have them illustrate the canticles with symbols and decorations. Encourage them to bring these home and use them as part of family or personal prayer.

9. Have the children make a "God box" in which they put slips of paper telling each time they said a prayer or did a special act of kindness during the Advent season. These will be their Christmas gift for Jesus. If possible, wrap up the box and bring it to the church to place it by the Nativity scene. (Check with the pastor first!)

1 0. Variation on the "God box"—Label and decorate the box. Then encourage the children to write down on a piece of paper their worries, anxieties, or fears and place them inside the box while asking for God's help. (Do explain that if there is an emergency or crisis that needs adult attention, they should talk about it with parents or teachers.)

## 10 Ways to Celebrate Christmas

1. Let the children share their favorite memories of this past Christmas. Especially note any ways in which they express gratitude for the more profound meaning of Christmas—the time and love shared with family and friends, and the way God is present to them through these people.

2. December 26 is the feast of St. Stephen, the first Christian martyr. This is a good opportunity to tell stories about the martyrs (to older children) and the early Church.

3. December 27 is the feast of St. John the Evangelist. Use this occasion to have a simple blessing for the class/family Bible, offering prayers of gratitude for this sacred book. Place the Bible in a prominent place with a decorative cloth and leave it in place throughout the Christmas season.

4. December 28 is the feast of the Holy Innocents. Offer prayers for children who are victims of violence, war, or abuse, and light a special candle for them throughout the Christmas season.

5. December 31 is the feast of the Holy Family. Have the class make cards or write letters to their families. Offer a class blessing over these before the students take them home.

6. January 1 is the feast of Mary, the Mother of God. Collect Marian prayers and devotions and share these with the class. Offer a special prayer to Mary using a traditional prayer (such as the Hail Mary or Memorare) or have the children compose their own.

7. January 4 is the feast of St. Elizabeth Seton, the first American saint. Tell the class her story or pick out the story of another saint to share. Offer a prayer of thanksgiving for these members of our church family.

8. For the feast of Epiphany (January 6), research ways that Orthodox churches celebrate this day. Remember these other Christian believers in your class/family prayers.

9. The feast of the Baptism of Jesus is the last Sunday of the Christmas season. Create a class mural of the life of Jesus. Hang this in a prominent place within the parish to share with other members of the community.

10. Kick off the new year with a list of hopes and wishes—for the children, their families, their parish, their school, and the world at large. Keep the list near the prayer corner and refer to it as the year unfolds, making note of any particular hopes and wishes that "come true."

## *10 Ways to Celebrate Lent*

1. Celebrate Mardi Gras by having a pancake meal. Traditionally, pancakes were eaten the night before Ash Wednesday in order to use up milk and butter, because it was forbidden to eat dairy products during the season of Lent.

2. Have the children research different kinds of crosses— such as the Latin, Maltese, Celtic, Jerusalem, Greek, Papal, and Anchor crosses. Older students can work together in groups to write reports and present them to the rest of the class. The students can also create reproductions of the crosses out of construction paper, tagboard, or other art materials.

3. Explain the Lenten traditions of fast and abstinence and then brainstorm a number of ways that the

class or family can "fast" from hurtful or destructive behavior during Lent. This might include "fasting" from calling each other hurtful names, interrupting one another, or having a negative attitude toward school. List one or two ways as a focal point and post the list in a predominant place in your classroom or home.

4.  Make a class examination of conscience, focusing on ways to live out the two parts of the Great Commandment—love of God and love of one another. Give each child a copy and ask them to review these alone or with their family each Friday during Lent.

5.  Hot cross buns are an old symbol of the Crucifixion. Make or purchase enough buns for each person in the class or family and savor their wonderful taste. Offer a prayer of thanksgiving to Jesus for his great sacrifice.

6.  Create class Stations of the Cross. Have the students work in groups to come up with ways to depict these in art, drama, or story form.

7.  Introduce the children to the concept of "pilgrimage." Have the older children research different sites for holy pilgrimages, such as Jerusalem or the Vatican. Create your own class or family "pilgrimage" by arranging to visit your diocesan cathedral or even by going to visit your own parish church.

8. Adopt a Lenten project. Ask the pastor or director of religious education for ways the children can assist the parish in its mission to reach out to those who are poor, sick, homebound, or otherwise in need.

9. Embark on a parish "cleanup" campaign, thus helping the parish in its efforts to get ready for the Easter season. Check with the pastor and maintenance person or committee to see what chores are doable for your age group.

10. Outline the Holy Week services for your children so that they can better understand this most sacred time in the church calendar. As a class, illustrate the highlights of each service of the Easter triduum—Holy Thursday, Good Friday, and the Easter Vigil/Easter Sunday. Include the symbols used for each one.

## 10 Ways to Celebrate Easter

1. To help the children understand Easter as a season vs. a day, create a basket of prayers. Obtain enough plastic Easter eggs to cover the number of times your class will meet between Easter and Pentecost. Write out a prayer or psalm that focuses on Easter themes of life and praise, and place a different one in each egg. Place eggs in a colorful Easter basket near the prayer table. Each time your class meets, open an egg and read your prayer together. You might also include a fun activity for the class to do together as well.

2. Have the children research the symbols of the Easter season—rabbit (life in abundance,) egg (birth and resurrection,) lamb (Jesus,) sunrise (new dawn, Christ's resurrection.) The students, individually or in a group, can present their findings to the class/family along with any appropriate artwork or symbols.

3. Discuss together the symbol of the "Easter outfit." This is probably derived from the ancient practice of baptism which took place at the Easter Vigil. Those being baptized shed their old clothes, entered a baptismal pool, and reemerged on the other side where they were clothed in a new white linen garment.

4. Have the children create an "Easter outfit" based on someone being "clothed in Christ." What would such a person wear? Colors? Fabrics? Special accents?

5. The Lent and Easter seasons are especially important times in the lives of those who are baptized or received into the Catholic Church at the Easter Vigil. Called "neophytes," these newest members of the Church are spending the Easter season reflecting upon their entry into the community of faith. Have your class make cards welcoming these new members to the parish and the Catholic faith.

6. There are numerous artworks focusing on the themes of the Easter season. Visit a local library and check out materials depicting the Resurrection, the

Ascension, and Pentecost. As you show these to the children, tell stories and examine how each artwork depicts the characters who are part of these stories.

7. Make a mural of the different appearances that Jesus made to his disciples after his resurrection. These include his appearance to Mary Magdalene in the garden (John 20:1–18), to the disciples in the locked room (John 20:19–23), to Thomas (John 20:24–29), to the seven disciples on the seashore (John 21:1–23), to the disciples on the road to Emmaus (Luke 24:13–35), and to the disciples on the mountain (Matthew 28:16–20). Display the mural in a prominent place in the parish so that others can enjoy it.

8. Read the story of Mary Magdalene's search for Jesus in the garden (John 20:1–18) and have the students act out the parts. Organize your own "search for Jesus" by hiding various symbols around the classroom/home or outside and letting the children find them.

9. Pick out various psalms of praise from Scripture and help the children memorize one or two lines from each. Use these as part of your prayers throughout the Easter season.

10. Give each student 10 small seeds in an envelope and ask them to think up 10 ways they can "plant" life in their home, school, parish, and in the world. Some

ideas might be to offer a smile instead of a complaint when asked to do something in school they would rather not do, or to make it a point to thank one person each day for something. Have them write these ideas out and place them in the envelope with their seeds. Place these in a basket on the prayer table. At the end of the Easter season, ask the students to make a picture or write an account of how their seeds "grew" during the past seven weeks.

## 10 Prayer Starters

1. Use photographs or artwork to help lay the groundwork for the theme of your prayer. Ask the children to consider how the picture makes them feel and what it leads them to pray for.

2. Use a story to lead into prayer. Choose one from your religious education materials or use one from a book. Make up your own story and relate a personal experience. Tie the story's themes to the focus of your prayer time.

3. Use gestures to help move the children into prayer. Ask them to set aside all papers and other objects (preferably out of sight and reach) and to fold their hands, close their eyes, and sit, stand, or kneel. Moving into prayer with the body signals a change in mood and focus. Whenever possible, model these gestures versus explaining them.

4. Use music, such as a simple song or a tape, to lead into prayer. The children can pick favorites or you can choose appropriate music to set a tone.

5. Use a clip from a film to help the children focus on the theme of prayer. For example, the "Circle of Life" sequence from the movie *The Lion King* (Walt Disney) might be a great way to start a prayer focused on creation and the goodness of God. Even a news clip can be useful as the children consider the many people who are in need of prayer and support.

6. Use newspaper stories as a way to introduce prayers centering around themes of peace and justice. This moves prayers of petition away from "gimme" experiences, and helps children learn about praying for the wider community.

7. Use a simple object from nature, such as a flower, a seed, or a piece of fruit, to help lead the children into prayers of praise for God's great gifts. Personal objects, such as photo albums, shoes, a favorite T-shirt or hat, can help the children offer prayers of thanksgiving for the simple gifts of life.

8. Use sacramental symbols, such as water, oil, bread, wine, a candle, or a cross, to help the children reflect upon and experience the importance of rite and ritual in the Church. Allowing students the opportunity to bless one another and themselves, to share bread together, to pass around a cross or a candle, gives

them a tactile way to better understand the importance of such symbols in the life of the Church.

9. Use an imaginative exercise to help the children relax and to make the transition from a lesson to prayer. Such an exercise can involve having the children close their eyes, relax through some deep breathing exercises, and then picturing themselves in a special place with Jesus. Speak softly, slowly, and clearly, and allow the students to move from one part of the reflection to the next without being rushed.

10. Use art to help the students move into prayer. Ask them to draw a picture or mold something out of a piece of clay that reflects the theme of your prayer. Gather these artworks around a table or in the middle of a circle as you continue with the rest of the prayer.

## *10 Prayer Ideas*

1. Create a prayer chain. Provide strips of colored construction paper and invite the children to write their prayer requests on them. Loop these together to form a chain. Use it throughout the year and watch it grow!

2. Light a candle. Invite the children to focus their attention on the flame and mentally repeat, "Jesus, you are my Light."

3. Read a parable. Ask the children to pick a person in the story and picture and imagine how it feels to really be that person.

4. Make a mandala. Help the children make their own and at prayer time, focus your attention on the center of the mandala.

5. Pray the Jesus Prayer. Invite the children to close their eyes and take a deep breath. As they inhale, mentally say "Je," and as they exhale, "sus." With each breath repeat the name *Jesus*.

6. The children can make a prayer corner in their room at home. It can be a little space with a prayer book, a Bible, a plant or flower, a favorite holy card or picture. This is their "special place to pray." Reinforce that we can pray always and anywhere.

7. Play mood music. Have the children close their eyes, be still, and listen. If a distraction comes to mind, instruct them to mentally say, "There's a thought about the soccer game, but right now I'm trying to just be still. I'll focus on the music." Distractions win when we fight them. Acknowledge them instead, and gently return to what you were doing.

8. Have the children create their own spontaneous prayer: "God loves me. I love God." "God, I love that you gave me my heart so I can love you and others."

9. When the children are worried, they can make a God box. They can write down their concerns and place them in the box. In this way, they turn over to God the things that are out of their control.

**1 0.** The children can picture God right with them, telling God about both their frustration and good stuff. Have them picture God with a giant tray and imagine putting their worries on the tray and God carrying them away.

## 10 Ideas for Rituals

1.  At the start of the year, ritualize the occasion by offering a simple classroom blessing. Gather the students into a circle and place all books and materials for the year in the center. Offer a simple prayer of blessing on all that you will be doing and learning together. Begin and end with the praying of the Sign of the Cross.

2.  At the beginning of the year, set up a small pottery bowl and make small squares of colored tissue paper available for writing down any ways the children wish to ask God for forgiveness. At any time they wish, they can write these down. They then tear the paper into small bits and place them in the bowl. At the end of the year, use this homemade confetti as part of a celebration of God's mercy and forgiving love.

3.  Ritualize the welcome-in part of your class each week in some special way. It might be standing by the door and greeting each child by name, or it might be asking all the students to greet each other in some appropriate way at the start of class.

4. In the same way, create a departure ritual. This might take the form of blessing the children as they leave by tracing a cross on their foreheads. In some way, let them know that they leave the room with your love and affection accompanying them.

5. Every time you share any type of food in the class/home, make sure to offer a prayer of grace.

6. Use seasons of the year as ways to incorporate ritual into your classroom/home structure. Mark the changing of the seasons of nature or the liturgical year by having the children join in the taking down and putting up of new decorations and symbols.

7. Have a once-a-month birthday celebration for the children whose birthdays fall within that time frame. Include a summer or "off month" as part of that celebration whenever you wish. Keep the celebration short, festive, and filled with prayer and good wishes for these children.

8. Whenever a student has experienced any sort of loss and wants to share it with the class, use a stone ritual to help lift the heavy burden from the student's shoulders. Pass a simple stone around a prayer circle and ask each student to help "lift away" the sadness that this student and the student's family feel at this time. Allow the stone to absorb the weight of the loss and place it on or near the prayer table.

**9.** Start each class or session with a bit of *"good news"* sharing—something good that the children have seen happen in their family, school, neighborhood, or in the world.

**10.** Establish a cleanup ritual that will help motivate the children to pitch in and help straighten up the room/home after an activity or before leaving. Sing a song or play some taped music to signal the time and pace for this activity.

## 10 Favorite Scripture Stories for Children in Primary and Intermediate Grades

1. ***Primary—The Story of Zacchaeus (Luke 19:1–10)*** This is a favorite story of children in grades 1–3. They love to point out that Zacchaeus was short! They also like stories in which Jesus is present with just one other person. It is difficult for them to get the message if there are too many people or nuances in the story.

2. ***Primary—The Creation Story (Genesis 1–2:4 or Genesis 2:4–25)*** Use a paraphrased or abridged version. Remember that children at this age are very concrete, so they take this story literally and remember it well.

3. ***Primary—The Infancy Narratives (Luke 2:1–14, Matthew 2:1–12, Matthew 2:13–15)*** Children remember well the stories of there being "no room at

the inn" and the coming of the visitors to Jesus' home—the shepherds and the magi. They love stories about Jesus' childhood.

4. **Primary—Jesus Blesses the Children (Matthew 19:13–15 or Mark 10:13–16)** This is obviously a warm and inviting story to young children who can easily visualize themselves being blessed by Jesus.

5. **Primary—Multiplication stories (for example, Feeding the Five Thousand—John 6:1–14)** Children tend to remember such stories and often become intrigued with the numbers.

6. **Intermediate—The Commandments (Exodus 20:1–17)** and **The Beatitudes (Matthew 5:1–11)** Fourth and fifth graders are very interested in keeping order and "rules," and so these accounts have a particular appeal for them. This age group is developing a sense of morality and they are able to recall and understand stories that relate to this.

7. **Intermediate—The Last Supper (Luke 22:14–20)** Children at this age are fascinated with the intrigue of Judas being included among those gathered. They wonder: If Jesus knew Judas was going to betray him, why was Judas included in this meal?

8. **Intermediate—The Prodigal Son (Luke 15:11–32)** This story of forgiveness is especially appealing to children this age, and they are very likely to view the son who

ran away and the forgiving father through the eyes of the "good" son. At this age, they like putting themselves into the story as they relate to particular characters and situations.

9. **Intermediate—Other forgiveness stories such as Peter's Denial of Jesus (Luke 22:54–62)** and **Zacchaeus (Luke 19:1–10)** These stores are appealing to children this age because they see these as "second chances"—opportunities to start over.

1 0. **Intermediate—Resurrection stories, in particular Mark 16:1–7** In this passage the women's story is doubted by the other disciples.

## 10 Favorite Scripture Stories for Youth in Middle/Junior High Grades

1. Children at this age can better appreciate Old Testament stories because they now have a developed historical sense and some exposure to various literary forms. Some favorites are: Creation (Genesis 1:1–31), Noah (Genesis 6:9–22), Abraham (Genesis 17:1–9, 21:1–6), Covenant with David (2 Samuel 7:1–17).

2. At this age, students are a bundle of insecurity. Therefore, they appreciate any of the stories that tell of the insecurities of others, such as Moses (Exodus 3–4:17) and Jeremiah (Jeremiah 1:4–10).

THE FAITH-FILLED CLASSROOM

3. Students view the story of the finding of Jesus in the Temple (Luke 2:41–52) as a story about Jesus and his parents, and they tend to appreciate Jesus' sense of "independence."

4. At this age, students like stories that depict Jesus as countercultural and antiestablishment, for example, Jesus throwing the money-changers out of the Temple (John. 2:13–25).

5. The Old Law-New Law challenges in chapters 5 and 6 of Matthew's account of the Gospel, appeals to the students' admiration of Jesus in standing up against the "establishment."

6. At this age, children are developing a social conscience. They enjoy stories that show Jesus' care for the poor and the outcast, for example, the parable of the rich man and Lazarus (Luke 16:19–31) and the widow's offering (Luke 21:1–4).

7. Children are searching for heroes at this age, and so they like stories that depict Jesus as such. These could include the account of the Transfiguration (Matthew 17:1–9) and any of the miracle stories.

8. For the same reason listed above, children at this age like to hear stories of Jesus' care for the sick and for those considered "outcasts," such as the healing miracles in chapter 9 of Matthew's account of the Gospel.

9. This age group also likes stories of forgiveness that offer a person "second chances." As with younger children, children of this age group appreciate the story of Peter's denial of Jesus (Luke 22:54–62). To them, it is seen as a story of friendship and loyalty.

10. The Acts of the Apostles appeals to children this age, and they like hearing about the depiction of an "ideal" way of being Church.

# –2–

## KEEPING THINGS INTERESTING

Children seem to learn better when the lessons are interesting and presented in new and novel ways. Creative parents and teachers are always looking for different ideas to enhance a specific topic, engage children in the process, and encourage hands-on experiences. The process of religious formation does not always depend on religion books. Learning can be fun and very exciting. Religious studies and doctrine can come alive for children, and they can put it into practice. There are creative ways to use music to develop a deeper understanding of prayer, values, and the messages this music sends to children. Videos can be used to help process some church teaching and enable children to scrutinize values and moral behavior in movies and everyday life. There are many places to visit and different ways for children to be of service to the church community. Certain doctrine must be memorized, and other teachings can be experienced firsthand. Variety is the spice of life.

## 10 Religious Education Field Trips

1. Take your child or the class to visit the diocesan cathedral. Arrange for a guided tour by someone who knows the history of the diocese and will be able to point out important features in the church and on the grounds.

2. Check with local museums and historical societies in the weeks preceding Christmas and Easter to inquire about special displays and exhibits they are planning that may be of interest to the children.

3. Plan a trip to a soup kitchen with the children outside of school hours. Do not arrive empty-handed! Ask the director if the children can bring homemade bread they made the night before or canned foods they

collected, to contribute to the kitchen's pantry. While at the soup kitchen, arrange for the children to have specific tasks—setting tables, pouring beverages, or even doing "K.P."

4. Your local library often has special holiday displays and will assemble a collection of materials for specific groups. For example, a class of junior high students might profit from seeing different forms of religious art throughout the ages.

5. Contact the rector or superior of a nearby seminary, monastery, motherhouse, or convent and ask for a tour of the facilities. This is a wonderful experience for students who are studying vocations. One of the young postulants or seminarians will often agree to give a tour and answer the students' questions.

6. Early in the year, check with high school and college theater departments and area community theater groups to see if a production of *Jesus Christ Superstar*, *Godspell*, or *Do Patent Leather Shoes Really Reflect Up?* is being planned. Tickets to student groups are often discounted as much as 50 percent.

7. Find out where the eucharistic breads used in your parish are made. Arrange a tour of the facility for a class of fifth graders who are studying about the Mass.

8. Work with the activity director of a nursing home to plan an event for the residents. With help, the children

can prepare a bingo party, a sing-along, a talent show, or even a play for the seniors and bring along refreshments to share at the end of the party.

9. If there is a synagogue in your area, contact the rabbi or the director of the Hebrew School to arrange for the children studying the Old Testament to tour the synagogue and ask questions about the Jewish faith today.

10. Plan a visit to an area Catholic cemetery with your students and one of your parish priests or deacons. Children often have many questions about Christian burial procedures and the rituals involved. This trip might include a visit to a funeral home.

## 10 Service Project Ideas

1. Based on Matthew 25:34–40 and the Corporal Works of Mercy, embark on a "scavenger hunt" food drive. Make sure that this is carried out under the supervision of adults. Arrange for food to be donated to the local parish or community food bank.

2. Another way to live out the Corporal Works of Mercy is to reach out to those who are imprisoned. Children of all ages can make cards to be sent to prison chaplains for distribution before or after religious services. Cards can include a prayer and reminders of God's love and goodness, and be sent on behalf of the

parish or school. (Check this out first with the pastor, principal, or director of religious education.)

3. Invite the children to do a closet clean-out and collect outgrown coats and clothes. Make sure to obtain parental permission before embarking on such a project. Clothes can be donated to local shelters for the homeless or to church or community agencies.

4. For junior high students, give out the following assignment: Go to the Goodwill store, and for less than six dollars, purchase an outfit for yourself. Take time afterward to share the results of their experience, and invite discussion about what the children learned from their experience. Share this information with parents and invite their observations of the process.

5. Assist a social ministry organization in the parish by having the children make sandwiches for homeless shelters and soup kitchens, help organize food shelves, or perform any other task that will put them in touch with the parish efforts to reach out to those who are poor.

6. Ask the pastor, director of religious education, or another member of the parish staff about having the children help out at an upcoming parish function. They can help prepare and serve food, assist in setup and decoration, or lend a hand in cleanup efforts.

7. Initiate a letter-writing project for the students to communicate their concerns about issues of justice to local and national leaders. These might range over a wide variety of areas, from issues on the environment to human rights and just policies for the poor.

8. Adopt a section of the church property to keep clean of trash and clutter. Check this out with the maintenance staff or committee.

9. (For older students) Sponsor a class bake sale, car wash, spaghetti dinner, or other fund-raiser and give the proceeds to an organization that helps at-risk youth.

10. Research the work of various parish committees or groups that focus on outreach and social ministry. Choose one and write a letter asking how the class might help in its efforts to carry out its work.

In general, the most successful service projects are "teachable moments" as well as being enjoyable. A park cleanup, for example, can be tied to a lesson on creation, and games and refreshments can be included.

## 10 Icebreakers

1. Cut index card pieces from construction paper into two pieces to make different puzzle shapes. Instruct

each student to pick a piece and try to find the person with the matching piece. Partners then sit together, introduce themselves, and share their favorite game, food, sport, or pastime.

2. Make sets of three cards on different religion topics. For example: three cards with the names of apostles, or three cards with the names of sacraments, or three cards naming different gospel miracles. Each child chooses a card and tries to find the two other children with cards having the same theme.

3. Ask the students: If you were an animal, what animal would you like to be? Have them explain their answers or have them pantomime the animal to see if others can guess what it is.

4. If the children all know each other, ask them to find a partner and do a "trust walk." One person closes their eyes and allows the partner to lead them around the room. Afterward, discuss how it felt to be led and how it felt to do the leading.

5. Tell a Bible story and ask for volunteers to act out a particular person or thing. For example, the Nativity scene could include Mary and Joseph, the shepherds and animals, the stable, and a star. Let each person, animal, or object tell what they saw that night. What gift or service did they give to the Holy Family or to Jesus?

6. Using Scripture story characters or objects, put the name of a biblical person or thing on an index card and cut it into puzzle pieces. The students then must search out the missing piece/pieces that make the word. For example: MA (on one piece) and RY (on a matching piece).

7. Write the name of a Christmas carol on two pieces of paper. Do this with several different carols and distribute the papers to the children. They must then find their song partner by humming the song and seeking out the person who shares the same song.

8. (Younger children) Make color-coded cards with a letter on each to spell out a religious name or reference. For example, five pink cards might spell J, E, S, U, S; three blue cards might spell G, O, D. The children pick a color and then find other cards with the same color and work together to figure out their word.

9. Do a birthday search. Each person calls out the month in which they were born, circulating the room until they find others with the same month. Continue in this manner until everyone has found (if possible) a birth-month group.

10. Have the group sit in a circle and start a sharing session by tossing a ball of yarn back and forth among the group. Begin by sharing something about yourself that the group might want to know, such as "My favorite food is . . ." or "I love to spend my spare time doing . . ." Holding on to the end of the string, toss the

ball to someone else and invite them to share in a similar way. They, too, hold on to their end of the yarn and toss the ball to another person. This continues until everyone has spoken and the group is "connected."

## 10 Ideas to Use When You Have Five Minutes Left in Class or on a Family Trip

1. Engage in a religion relay. Start by saying a word such as JESUS. The next person in the circle or row must respond with a religious term or name starting with the ending letter of that word, such as SACRAMENT. The next person then gives another word starting with the end letter, T. Play continues in this way as quickly as possible until all the children have had a chance to respond.

2. Play Scripture Scrabble on the chalkboard or on paper. Start with a word such as SACRAMENTS. A volunteer builds on one letter: for example, they may write CHRIST down from the C, as in Scrabble. Continue as long as desired.

3. Play Notable Numbers by asking the children to tell about a number they learned about from the Bible or in connection with the teaching of the Church. Examples: 3—Trinity, 7—sacraments, 10—Commandments, 5,000—people fed.

4. Play Scripture Jeopardy by making a statement and asking the students to frame the corresponding

question. For example: "I baptized Jesus in the Jordan River."—"Who is John the Baptist?" Or "The sacrament that only deacons, priests, and bishops receive."—"What is Holy Orders?"

5. Have the children pantomime a gospel miracle story. One person takes the part of Jesus and acts out a miracle. The children must identify the miracle and tell the story.

6. Read or tell a short biography of a saint or someone people consider a "modern-day saint," such as Mother Teresa or Archbishop Oscar Romero. Ask the children how we can be like that person in our life.

7. Have a Bible search. Give the students a Scripture chapter and verse to look up. Individual students or teams search for the passage and the first person or team who finds it reads the passage out loud.

8. Share good news together. Have a scroll ready for use each week and take a few minutes to write down any examples the students have witnessed of someone living out the gospel message. One week might focus on good works; another might focus on unselfish acts.

9. As a way to keep collage pictures on hand, take a few minutes to have students cut out pictures from magazines or newspaper and place them in plastic bags. This will be useful when an upcoming project calls for such materials.

**10.** Play Hangman on the chalkboard, using biblical vocabulary words.

## 10 Ways to Use Music

1. Use simple instruments to add to any group singing. Include shakers, drums, and so on, made by the learners.

2. Sing blessings instead of saying them. Make up your own tunes or invite the children to do so, or use a familiar nursery rhyme or other simple tune and change the words.

3. Use taped music, such as Gregorian chant, classical music, or simple instrumental pieces to help the children become more reflective in their prayer.

4. Taped music can also be used as background music as the children are working on individual or group activities. Such music is often calming and relaxing.

5. Use "mood" music as a backdrop when you are reading a story or during a dramatic activity.

6. Sing-along tapes are a great way to stimulate singing, especially for adults who don't feel quite comfortable leading the song all alone.

7. Invite the students to bring in music to share with the rest of the class. Explain that they need to give it to you in advance so that you have a chance to listen to it first. Then, if you deem it appropriate, ask the

students to share with the class why this particular piece of music is important to them.

8. Use music to accompany movement in prayer. For example, to move in a reverential way from one place to another, use taped or sung music as a backdrop for the processional tone you are setting.

9. Make use of psalm responses that are sung during the Sunday liturgies. Invite a parish musician to class to help the students learn to sing the responses.

10. Use rounds and divide the children into two or three groups to sing them.

## *10 Ways to Use Video*

1. Use a clip from a popular movie or TV show to start a discussion. Carefully cue the clip to its starting point, and know exactly where you want to end it. Have discussion questions ready in advance.

2. Start prayer with a short video or clip. This might be something poetic and artistic, or something that invites the children to reflect upon human need and suffering.

3. Clips from news programs can be a good way to help the children use topics of current local or national interest and to spur on teaching about the Church's stand on contemporary issues.

4. Start a catalog of video ideas. When watching a particular film or video, consider if it might be usable in the classroom or home as a way to further open up the message of Christ to your children.

5. Start, stop, and replay videos or clips as a way to help the students go beyond superficial answers and observations. You might freeze a frame and ask them what is going to happen next, or rewind the tape and show it again, asking the children to watch for particular scenes or watch it from a particular perspective.

6. Use video to help the children become more media-savvy. Ask them to critique scenes by asking what the message of the video is. For example, showing a few TV commercials might help the children to see that the message is, "If you want to be happy, buy our product." Then ask them to think more deeply about that question. Is it true? Is this what Jesus tells us we need to be happy?

7. Many sitcoms on television base their story lines around a particular moral dilemma being faced by one or more of the characters. Clips from shows that are appropriate for the age level you are teaching could be ways to help the children discuss alternative responses. For example, do they agree with the character's responses to the situation? Why or why not?

8. Link this activity to the above activity. The children could be asked to rescript a story in order to make a

character's actions and responses more consistent with a Christian way of acting.

9. Ask the children to watch for specific things when showing them a video clip. It might be the way something is said, or how it is filmed. Encourage them to become more deeply engaged in the process rather than being passive viewers.

10. At the beginning of the year, have the students make a list of their favorite TV shows and movies. Ask them to explain why they have made these choices. Keep the lists and redistribute them at the end of the year. Would they make any changes to the list or to their responses? Why or why not?

## 10 Quick Crafts for Children in Intermediate Grades

1. Have the children make "stained-glass windows" depicting the sacraments, using markers and vellum— a paper architects use. This slick, translucent paper is easy to work with and creates a wonderful effect when displayed on a window.

2. Make "pop-up" cards for Mother's Day. Have the children cut three-inch hearts and a thin red strip from red craft paper. Show them how to fold the strip accordion-style to create a small "spring." Glue one end of the "spring" to the card and the other end to the back of the heart. Invite the children to write personal messages to their moms inside the card.

Fold the card, decorate the outside, and place it in a book to keep it flat. When the card is opened, the heart "pops up." (If their mother is deceased, have the children write what they would like to say to their mom, e.g., "I love you and miss you," and keep the letter, or write a letter to their caregiver who may be "mothering" them now.)

3. Invite groups of sixth graders to make an Old Testament time line with markers and white shelf paper. Have each group illustrate the major Old Testament people and events they have studied during the year. The time lines can be added to throughout the year.

4. Near Ash Wednesday, read the story of Noah to the class. Give the children small rocks and tempera paints. Instruct them to paint rainbows on the rocks as a reminder to keep their Lenten promises. Invite them to keep their rocks in a prominent place at home where they can see them each day and recall their significance.

5. As a reminder to live out their baptismal calling, have the children trace the outline of one of their feet onto construction paper. Ask them to write their name on one side. On the reverse side, instruct them to write one or more ways in which they will "walk with Jesus" in their daily lives.

6. Have the children make candleholders from soup cans. Direct them to cut a piece of colored construction paper to cover the outside of the can.

Then have them decorate the paper with pictures related to what they are studying in religion: Mary, the Beatitudes, the Holy Spirit. When finished, have them glue it to the can. Supply a votive candle for each child to use in their candle holder.

7. Encourage the students to create thumbprint pictures illustrating original stories about living the Ten Commandments. Divide the class into small groups, distribute unlined paper, and give each group stamp pads in a variety of colors. Have the youngsters draw panels on the paper and use thumbprints to represent the people in their stories. Be sure to have moist towelettes on hand for cleanup.

8. A paper plate mobile can be used to feature the sacraments, the Ten Commandments, or other important areas of our faith. Give each child a paper plate and demonstrate how to roll it into a cone shape and staple it. Then invite the children to decorate the cone. Have them design and make symbols from tagboard that relate to the theme. Using a hole puncher and yarn, help them attach the symbols to the bottom of the cone. Tie a long piece of yarn to the top of the cone for hanging.

9. Help the children recall the importance of the fish symbol as an identifying sign for early Christians. Make several fish patterns. Fold a piece of paper in half to make a card and have the children trace the

fish pattern onto one side. Have them print the name JESUS inside the fish and decorate it by gluing yarn pieces along the edges. On the back of the card, have them copy the word ICHTHUS. Explain that this word means "fish" in Greek and that it is derived from the first letter of the Greek words meaning "Jesus Christ, Son of God, Savior."

**10.** Give each student a piece of tagboard, glue, and small pieces of yarn. Brainstorm various Christian symbols the students might create with the yarn, such as a cross, a rainbow, or a Chi Rho. Have the students decide on a symbol, draw it on tagboard, and glue enough yarn pieces on it to completely fill in the symbol. When the glue has dried, have them place a piece of unlined paper over the symbol. Using the side of a crayon, show them how to transfer the design by rubbing over it until its image appears on the top paper. Then have the students write a message related to the symbol on the first page. As an example, they might write, "God keeps his covenant with us always."

# –3–

# *IDEAS FOR THE CLASSROOM*

A formal religious education program is usually taught in a classroom. Teachers, as coworkers with parents, continue the process of nurturing the religious formation of children. Organized teachers with well-orchestrated religion lessons and class management skills can create a pleasant environment where a group of same-age children can learn. In this classroom setting, children need a predictable environment, as well as definite limits that help provide a sense of safety and create this atmosphere for learning. Certain rules and different organizational techniques can help eliminate behavioral problems and enable this special time to be stress free and one of sharing together. Hopefully, this will be a totally different experience from their everyday studies in school. Teachers try, through example, to create a loving, Christian ambiance where children can learn about their religion and how to be active participants in their church community. The reality is that children will be children, so we hope the following suggestions will be helpful resources for you to use in your classroom experience.

## 10 Tips for the First Day of Class

1. For younger students, make stand-up name "tents" with their names printed boldly on both sides of the tent. Not only can you see their names when they speak, but so can the other members of the class.

2. Have the students in third through eighth grades make their own name tags, using a variety of materials, such as construction paper, felt-tip markers, scissors, pieces of yarn and fabric, sequins, glitter, and glue. Encourage the students to make a name

tag that tells something about who they are. Allow time for sharing when finished.

3. Take individual pictures of each student in the class or a group shot. If you are lucky enough to have access to an instant camera, you can make a class collage immediately. If not, have the film developed and work on a class poster during your next session.

4. Make a birthday chart for your class and plan some easy way to celebrate these special days. In lieu of sending edible treats to class on birthdays, you might want to encourage parents to donate a book or video to your religious education resource center instead.

5. Plan a prayer service built around the theme of "blessings." As a part of the prayer service, bless the students' books after they have been distributed. Use holy water from church to bless the books and the students.

6. Establish class rules with the students. Write the rules out in positive, rather than negative, terms. For example, the rule "No interrupting" can be better stated, "We will listen when someone else is talking and wait our turn to speak."

7. Select an area of the classroom to use as a prayer area. Set up a small table (a folding tray table works well) and cover it with a cloth appropriate to the season. Decorate the table with a Bible stand, Bible,

crucifix, statue, candles, or a bowl of holy water. Older students can sign up to take turns preparing the table with religious objects from home that have special meaning for them.

8. Plan a "get-acquainted" activity. Have the students interview one another in pairs and then "introduce" their interviewee to the class. Or, play a game in which the students list their "favorites" in different categories—food, television shows, family events, hobby, sport, and so on. Have the students form small groups to compare answers. Or, have them make descriptive acrostics, using the letters in their name to tell something about themselves. Sue might describe herself as a sports lover, unusual, and enthusiastic.

9. Be ready for tears from the youngest primary students. Do not force those who are reluctant to come into the classroom alone; instead, encourage the parent who has accompanied the child to stay until the child's fears are calmed.

10. Watch the clock. Wrap up your lesson five minutes before the bell rings so that you have time to calmly distribute papers, make announcements, and dismiss your class in an orderly fashion. Never try to squeeze a last-minute prayer into the last second. Before you let the class go, ask them to verbally tell you one specific thing they learned in your session.

## 10 Keys to Positive Discipline

1. Use a seating chart. This gives the students their own "place" in the classroom and makes them accountable for what happens in and around that place.

2. Never yell to get the students' attention. Instead, wait in silence until the class is quiet again. Then use a quiet tone of voice to continue the lesson.

3. Never force a youngster to apologize in front of the class. The apology will be only grudgingly offered and all you will have gained is an enemy.

4. Do not punish the class for one student's actions—shame is a poor motivator for improved behavior.

5. Do not shoot butterflies with machine guns. In other words: do not overreact. Do not allow incidents to accumulate to the point where you finally blow up. Handle discipline problems as they occur.

6. Praise good behavior each time you "catch" a student acting positively. Be specific. For example: "Kim, it was thoughtful of you to help pick up the crayons Jake spilled."

7. Tell the students your expectations. Work with the class to develop a short list of rules—no more than five. Enforce the rules consistently.

8. Take the time to speak to students privately about their misbehavior. Allow students to tell you their side of the story.

9. Make sure your program has a policy for students who act up in class. At what point should students be sent to the office? At what point are parents to be called?

10. Maintain a sense of humor. When something funny happens in class, laugh instead of trying to shush the group. Laughing shows that you are human, and it is a great energizer for the entire class.

## 10 Classroom Management Ideas

1. Be prepared to teach. Know your lesson inside and out. The better organized you are, the smoother your class will go.

2. Plan to spend one and a half times as long preparing your lesson as you will devote to teaching it. A good rule of thumb: Set aside 90 minutes to prepare for a one-hour class. You can easily space your prep time out over several days.

3. Plan to arrive at church or school 30 minutes before class begins. This gives you time to organize your resources, set up audiovisual equipment, read any memos from your director, and take a deep breath before the students arrive.

*Ideas for the Classroom*

**4.** Be ready for your students' arrival and personally greet them by name at the door. This tells them that you are happy to see them and ready for a great class.

**5.** Lay out any supplies or resources you need before the students arrive. This will save you valuable class time hunting for a storybook you want to read or an extra set of markers.

**6.** Never leave your class alone or unsupervised. Never.

**7.** In planning your lesson, be specific. For example, do not just plan to pray. Plan what kind of a prayer the class will pray, how you will pray it, where you will pray it, and when you will pray.

**8.** Be realistic about time. Can your students readily finish the arts and crafts activity that you planned? Or will they be frustrated at their inability to finish it because they have to move on to another part of the lesson?

**9.** Set a time limit for each segment of the lesson and stick to it. Otherwise, at the end of class, you will be forcing the students to race through your final activities and they may miss the entire point of the lesson.

**10.** Change activities frequently during class. It keeps the students from experiencing "brain lock" and helps them stay interested. Move from a large-group activity to small-group discussions. Get them out of their desks for prayer or the reading of a story.

## 10 Family Take-Home Ideas

1. Suggest TV/video ideas that are suitable for family viewing. With so much media bombarding families these days, ideas on good, wholesome, and value-laden resources are much appreciated.

2. Provide prayers to use at the family table or for morning or evening use—blessings for bedtime or departing for school or work, for example.

3. Write short (one-paragraph) updates or information about the religious education program and class the child is in. Overloading parents with information is counter-productive. Make every take-home piece count!

4. Supply a list of books for family reading or parenting ideas. Parents often look to the parish for ideas on spirituality and inspiration, so share your resources with them.

5. Suggest family internet sites that you have previewed. As use of the internet continues to escalate, another valuable resource is that of specific ideas on sites that are family-friendly. Set up a network among parents so that site suggestions can be shared among families.

6. Provide information on parish family events. Just because information about the event appeared in the bulletin or was announced at Mass does not mean everyone got the message. Send home

information and underscore why you think this is an event worth attending.

7. Give seasonal tips and suggestions for celebrating sacred and secular holidays. Keep these short, usable, and practical.

8. Provide a family activity suggestion each month.

9. Present information on the spiritual development of children. Your religious education series is most likely to have some valuable information about the different stages of emotional, psychological, and spiritual development of children. Share these ideas with parents in the form of short "blurbs" sent home on a regular basis.

10. Write notes of affirmation and gratitude. We are often quick to tell parents when things go wrong. When is the last time you let parents know you appreciate their involvement, their generosity, their presence—and their children?

## 10 Time-Savers

1. Look over an entire unit versus just planning your lessons chapter by chapter. This gives you a longer-range view of what lies ahead and will enable you to prioritize the most important parts of your lesson plans a month or so in advance.

2. Evaluate often. Assess how things went at the end of each class by writing down your thoughts and reactions. Make notes about the following week while they are still fresh in your mind.

3. Use a single box, complete with file folders or other organizational tools, to carry your lessons and materials in and out of class. Keeping things in one place makes it easier to plan and to lay your hands on the most important items.

4. Prioritize! Look at your entire lesson plan first, for example, and pick out the two most important pieces of it. This is what should get the bulk of your attention and energy. Lesser pieces can be planned later or let go of.

5. Use "invisible time" well. This is the time we spend waiting in doctors' offices or after kids' sporting events, before everyone's ready to go. Bring along a folder of "to read" items that can be completed in small time chunks.

6. Go "off-line" while planning or completing critical tasks. Let the answering machine take your phone calls so that you focus your attention on the task at hand.

7. Learn to say no! If this is difficult the first time around, at least forestall requests for your commitment by seeking out the opinions of people whose lives will be impacted by your saying yes to one

more thing. This might be a spouse, coworker, or child. Also, block out the time commitments that saying yes will involve, so that you can make an informed decision.

8. Plan daily "joy breaks"—small breaks that allow you to rejuvenate heart, soul, body, and mind.

9. Delegate!!!

10. Simplify. Do not let projects get out of hand and overwhelm the topic matter that needs the most attention. It is easy to get caught up in minor details and to lose touch with the bigger picture.

## 10 Tips for Dealing with Students with Special Needs

1. Look at how to make your classroom wheelchair-accessible. Special needs students want to belong and to be in class with their peers whenever possible.

2. Students with learning disabilities may be a part of your class. Investigate their abilities and try to adjust the lesson to help them succeed. This may mean asking them to repeat back to you what they heard, for example, so that you can be sure they understood directions for a particular activity.

3. Acknowledge your own feelings about children with special needs and then spend some time helping the students heighten their perception and acceptance.

4. Students with an attention deficit disorder or similar conditions may be labeled disruptive if you do not know their classification. Talk to parents, consult with the director of religious education or the principal, and find other ways to learn about their particular needs. Make it a goal to help them succeed in loving and learning their religion and their relationship with God.

5. Enlist the help of a volunteer aide to help out with special projects or to work with a small group, including students with special needs. This is a great way to provide one-on-one help to particular students.

6. Adapt your lesson so the student may "quietly" take it home and finish it with parental help.

7. The National Catholic Office for Persons with Disabilities, P.O. Box 29113, Washington, D.C. 20017-0113, telephone (202) 529-2933, has many resources available for Catholics with disabilities.

8. There are Special Needs Catechist Guides that provide adapted lesson plans to be used in mainstream religious education classes, for grades one to five. Published by Silver Burdett & Ginn, Religion Division, 299 Jefferson Road, P.O. Box 480, Parsippany, NJ 07054-0480, telephone (201) 739-8000.

9. *Guidelines for the Celebration of the Sacraments with Persons with Disabilities* is now available through the

U.S. Catholic Conference, 1-800-235-8722. If you are teaching a class that is preparing for a sacrament, this is an excellent resource.

10. *Guidelines for the Celebration of the Sacraments with Persons with Disabilities* is available in large print and audiotape from the National Catholic Office for Persons with Disabilities, same phone number as in item 7.

# –4–

## STRESS-BUSTERS AND SOUL-BUILDERS

As children grow in their faith and begin to understand more about their religion, they will become more aware that all of this growth is grounded in love: God's unconditional love for us and our love of God. They will also realize that we have a commandment, a call from God, to love our neighbor as ourselves. This command carries a very forceful message that we must take care of ourselves physically, mentally, spiritually, and emotionally. Sometimes it is very easy to love others, do things for them, and not really love ourselves. Self-esteem, taking care of our souls and bodies, may be seen as selfish, and very hard to do. Yet, this is a command and also a lifelong process.

We cannot love others without loving ourselves. So, if we continually give and give to the damage of self, we are negating the giving process, and we are not doing what we were asked to do. This is a challenge that all of us—children and adults—must choose to answer for our better health. No one can do this for us. We must choose to maintain a balance between self-care and "burning out." We need to learn healthy ways to deal with our busy schedules, the distress and the gamut of feelings we experience each day.

Jesus showed us how to achieve that healthy balance. Jesus took time to be silent, to go off and pray and refill his cup. He also knew when to teach, to preach, and to do things for others. We, too, can be instruments of God's healing love and service to others, while we take time and space to pray, to soothe and nurture our body and soul so we will be refilled for the journey through life.

## 10 Ways to Feed Your Soul

1. Listen to a favorite piece of music and savor its beauty.

2. Take a walk around a park, nature trail, or your own neighborhood. Slow down enough to appreciate the goodness of God's creation.

3. Compile a list of things you can do in five minutes or less that can be used as mini soul-feeders within the course of a day. These might include reading from a book of cartoons, writing a thank-you note, savoring the taste of a candy bar or cup of tea. Keep the list handy and use it each day.

4. Spend an afternoon in a library or bookstore browsing through books. Make a list of books you would like to read and start on it!

5. Check out a favorite, uplifting video, make a favorite snack, and settle down for a few hours of relaxation.

6. Write a love letter to a spouse, friend, family member, or God.

7. Visit a place of beauty—an art museum or arboretum or botanical garden, for example. Visit it alone or with someone you love.

8. Sit in stillness for five minutes with a lit candle before leaving your house in the morning or before going to bed.

9. Read one psalm slowly and reflect upon its meaning in your life.

10. Spend one week or month composing daily prayers of thanksgiving. When the time is up, read all of them over and appreciate anew the blessings of life. Save them for reading over when facing difficult days.

## 10 Midyear Pickups for Teachers

1. Skim over the remaining chapters in your teacher's manual and reassess where you are headed for the remainder of the year.

2. Go over what you have already covered for the year by leafing through your teacher's manual. Make particular note of what worked for you and congratulate yourself.

3. Plan a midyear treat for yourself and for your class. Arrange for a field trip, read a special story, plan a simple celebration, and have some fun together.

4. Change your classroom environment. Redo bulletin boards, prayer corners, or seating arrangement. Enlist your students' help in giving your room a new, fresh look.

5. Watch a video or read a book or article that will help you learn a new skill as a teacher.

**6.** Delegate more responsibility to your teacher assistant or to any other volunteers who might be helping you out. This is a good time to affirm their work, and to ease your own workload a bit.

**7.** Call five parents and tell them something great about their child and how much you enjoy having him or her in your class.

**8.** Read over any cards or letters given to you by your students and remember what makes each of them so special.

**9.** Create a "wonderful things" file, and place such letters and notes inside of it.

**10.** Make a list of five ways you have become a better teacher since the beginning of the year. Leave room to add five more at the end of the year. Place it in your "wonderful things" file.

## 10 Stress Relievers for Children

**1.** Lead the children through this exercise: Sit quietly, up straight, close eyes or stare at a spot on the wall, take a deep breath (as deep as is comfortable), hold, and then exhale slowly. Picture blowing out distress and releasing tension. Repeat slowly two or three times.

2. Play a recording of soft music. Ask the children to listen and imagine themselves in a very calm, beautiful setting, peaceful and safe (on a beach, a mountain). Let them enjoy the picture this creates in their mind.

3. Invite the children to stand at attention. Ask them to lift their right arm and left leg (as if marching), then the right leg and left arm. Slowly alternate side to side. This is a form of kinesiology, to balance left and right brain function and help one relax and be rejuvenated.

4. Invite the children to sit on a chair, tighten their arm muscles, make a fist, then release it and relax. Then have them tighten and release their leg muscles. Repeat this two or three times, if the children are physically able.

5. Instruct the class to stand while the leader names the following movements: Be a **rag doll** (students flop arms and become very limp). Be a **tree** (arms out, body sways). Be an **eagle.** Do the **"twist."** Play **"Simon Says."**

6. Use a tape or sing a tune. Encourage the children to let the body move and release tension. Have them do the "Chicken Dance," "Macarena," "Alley Cat," "Hokey Pokey," "Hawaiian," or "Rock and Roll."

7. Drawing pictures can also help the children relax. Using large pieces of paper and crayons, allow the

children to "free draw," or scribble with no set pattern. You can also use a chalkboard.

8. Have the children write a letter to a person or about a situation that has caused stress. Writing a journal or letter (that does not have to be mailed) can reduce stress and can be done privately. Have them write as if speaking directly to the person and then rip the letter up or save it. Then if they want to, they can write another letter, or go and talk to the person.

9. Ask the children to close their eyes and imagine themselves going down an elevator or escalator. Have them count as they take a few deep breaths—5, 4, 3, 2, 1. Suggest that they mentally repeat a word or phrase, such as *Jesus, peace, love, I'm safe.*

10. Have the children play basketball, ride a bike, run, do something physical. This is a good way to release stress. Some children play computer games to release their stress.

## 10 Ways to Enhance Self-esteem in Children and in Ourselves

Self-esteem is a lifelong job, and we must continue to acknowledge that God, the "Potter," formed and shaped this very special creation. We are not perfect, nor are we supposed to be. Each one of us is a "10." This means there is not another soul like me in the universe. God loves me and made me special with my gifts and talents that make me, *me*.

1. Make a sign: "I am made in the image and likeness of God." Put the sign over a mirror and ask each child to look in the mirror and read the sign out loud. Encourage yourself and the students to do this many times a day at home or school. It is the truth!

2. Make a sign: "I am lovable and capable." Tape this on the bathroom or bedroom mirror. Every time you look in the mirror, read the sign out loud. It is also true.

3. Make a sign: "I am unique and special." Decorate it and carry it with you every day. Read it often. By repeating these affirmations you can enhance your self-esteem.

4. Help the children understand "unique" and "different." *Unique* means one of a kind, a special creation of God. *Different* means I have blue eyes and brown hair, and you have brown eyes and black hair. My body is made the way my DNA and genetic structure are supposed to be, for me. Celebrate "me-ness."

5. Do not put a child down in front of others. Do not call a child bad names, like stupid or dumb, or say, "You can't do anything right." Research studies have found that negativity gets recorded on our minds, and we believe it as if it were true. What messages do you say to yourself that make you feel bad? Cancel these

from your thoughts! Delete them and replace them with an affirmation, **"I am lovable."**

6. Name five things you like about yourself. Write them down. Say them often.

7. Name three special gifts you have. Write them down. Say them often. You will not get a big head. The person who must put others down has very low self-esteem.

8. Write yourself a love letter. Include things you like about yourself and your gifts. Put your letter in an envelope and mail it to yourself. Upon its arrival, read it, save it, put it on your mirror. Write yourself a love letter frequently and see the new "good things" to add about yourself.

9. We all try to please others. Try not to judge the children, even with praise. Instead, ask the children how they feel about the work accomplished. Help them to look within and praise themselves for a job well done. This will help them to believe in themselves and not look to others for their praise and approval.

10. Our self-talk either builds us up or pulls us down. Do not speak ill of yourself. If there is a behavior you do not like, you can work on changing it. It is a lie to put yourself down and deny the beautiful, lovable, capable, unique, and special creation that you are. God made you and God only does good work.

## 10 Tips to Help Children/Youth Express Their Feelings

1. Explain that feelings are good and just as important as sleeping and eating. We feel happy, sad, mad, scared. Give examples of when Jesus expressed his feelings.

2. Use everyday examples to help the children understand that we experience many losses in our lives. People die, get sick, or divorce; there are floods, accidents, fires, and disasters. Nevertheless, life goes on. Naming and expressing our feelings helps us. Acknowledge that feelings are normal. Listen to the children.

3. Encourage the children to write get-well or congratulation cards. After a death, have them write a letter of condolence to their classmate and the family. Writing to others helps to acknowledge that our thoughts and prayers are with others. It can also help children to develop empathy.

4. After a death or a divorce in the family, children may not want to talk about it, so the adult may ask the child in private to share how they are doing. Acknowledge the loss.

5. Encourage the children to talk about feelings to a trusted person or write out their feelings in a journal.

6. Be alert to children who are sad or depressed. Ask them to share their story with you, if they wish. Some sadness or depression is normal after a major loss.

7. Let the children know that you are a caring, empathetic listener. If a child's feelings are chronic and intense, alert the child's family. The child may need professional help.

8. Read gospel stories that express appropriate and intense feelings. The death of Lazarus or of Jarius' daughter, or Jesus in the garden or in the Temple are good examples. Discuss how people felt in the stories and why.

9. Help the children understand that when we love intensely, we will grieve and feel pain. We cannot run or hide from it. If we deal with what we feel, we can heal.

10. Naming, expressing, and dealing with feelings in an appropriate way helps to heal life's hurts and hold those we love in our hearts and memories forever.

# IDEAS FOR CATECHETICAL LEADERS

The Council of Vatican II called for an update of the Church. The Council Fathers strongly encouraged the laity, as the people of God, to become more and more actively involved in the life of their parish. Many parents and teachers answered this request. Some became eucharistic ministers, lectors at liturgy, directors of religious education, financial advisers, and volunteers on all different levels and aspects of parish life. All were working together as Church, in the continuing process of the religious formation of children and adults.

Some parents and teachers became involved by becoming catechists, teaching classes in the religious education program for the children. Besides the formal teaching of doctrine, these programs continue to build a bridge between the home and the parish.

The director or catechetical leader continues to encourage new parishioners to become involved in the program by teaching, sharing at-home projects with the children, being a chaperone on a class trip, or volunteering their services when and if they are able.

To ensure that the process of religious formation is an ongoing reality, it takes the continued cooperation of all those involved in the life of the children. As the children continue to grow in age and wisdom, it is the joint responsibility of the people of God to encourage the children to grow in their faith.

### 10 Tips for Recruiting Volunteers

1. Make it a point to meet all new families entering your program. Invite them to get involved once they are settled into their new home. Follow up with a phone call several weeks later.

2. Ask current volunteers to each recommend a friend or neighbor. Encourage them to make the initial contact with the person they recommended.

3. Showcase volunteers in a variety of ways: list the religious education staff's names in the bulletin on Sundays devoted to honoring those who teach; write a monthly "Meet Our Catechists" feature article highlighting one religious education teacher per month for the bulletin; run a photo of a religious education gathering—a planning meeting, a Christmas party, or a day of retreat—in a newsletter.

4. Recruit all year—not just in August when you are desperate. Get out and meet parents who arrive early to pick up their kids from classes; be present at any "newcomer" events the parish sponsors. In short, be visible in the parish.

5. In the spring, sponsor a "Religious Education Recruitment Sunday." Invite different teachers to speak briefly at Sunday liturgy about the experiences they have had in sharing their faith with young people and inviting parishioners to consider joining this important ministry.

6. Let people know your needs. Do not just beg for catechists. Be specific. Advertise that you need two fifth grade teachers, one first grade instructor, and three junior high volunteers.

7. Have a poster contest for the children. Invite them to work in teams or on their own to create recruitment posters for catechists. Invite your board of education to judge the contest and award decent prizes. Display

the completed posters in the church vestibule, the parish hall, and anywhere parishioners gather.

8. **Be up front about the commitment.** How much time is required? How many training meetings will be held? How many class sessions are scheduled? How much help can a new religious education teacher expect from you and your staff? Create a job description for each volunteer position.

9. **Design clever ads.** A banner headline—such as, "There Are 8,760 Hours in an Average Year. Here's a Great Way to Spend 78 of Those Hours"—will get more attention and interest than an ad that shouts, "Religious Education Teachers Needed."

10. **Be good to your volunteers.** Send personal birthday, Christmas, and Easter cards to every volunteer. Praise every good work you see or hear about. Thank them for their commitment and dedication. Treat them the way you would want to be treated.

## 10 Ways to Involve Parents

1. Create specific volunteer opportunities that will use a variety of talents. Brainstorm ideas with catechists; define tasks and time lines.

2. Create a monthly newsletter. Along with giving parents essential information, it can also contain

short highlights from each class. Recruit a few parents to compile it and format it (computer buffs might love this type of thing!).

3. Form a family advisers' board. Ask three or four parents with varying family backgrounds to be part of this. Use them to assess program plans and implementation, to critique promotional tools, to suggest ways to further involve parents and to be sensitive to families, and to evaluate religious education programs and resources.

4. Make it a priority to phone five parents per month in order to hear their ideas and listen to their concerns. Such interviews can give you valuable insights into parent needs and perceptions, and introduce you to people you might not have otherwise met.

5. Send home regular family resource ideas. Keep them "fridge friendly" by making sure they are short and practical for sticking on the family refrigerator door. Parenting ideas, thoughts on forming faith in the home, prayer ideas, and resources are all welcome ways to reinforce the role of the parents in the building of faith in their children.

6. Knock down barriers to involvement. Do not assume that people do not come to programs or volunteer to help because they do not care. Some parents are unable to leave their homes, for example, because they might be caring for an elderly parent or a sick or

disabled child. Work with the parish's social concerns committee to set up respite care so that these people are freed up from such responsibilities once in a while in order to be involved in the parish community.

7. Be sensitive to varying degrees of religious involvement at home. Try to provide resources that will appeal to a family with an ecumenical or interfaith background.

8. Coordinate your planning with other parish staff members so that a few families are not overburdened with too many invitations to volunteer.

9. Consider "chunking" volunteer assignments, asking people to serve as class aides, for example, for a monthlong period vs. year-round. This makes the volunteer commitments for parents easier to do.

10. Set up lines of communication between yourself and parents. When and how can they reach you? At the beginning of the year, ask them for their thoughts on how to best communicate with them.

## 10 Ways to Promote Your Programs

1. When writing any announcements, brochures, flyers, or other promotion for your program, think **features** and **benefits.** What will draw people? What will they gain from the experience? Why would they *want* to come?

2. Keep announcements short and sweet. Avoid wordiness and do not lay guilt on anyone for not attending. Ask a trusted friend or adviser to read over all promotional pieces and invite honest feedback.

3. Define clearly the time commitment involved for someone coming to the program. Is it a weekly program? Monthly? Occasional? How long does each session last? What alternatives are offered for those who are interested but cannot attend with the schedule as is? Will it be repeated? Video- or audio-taped? Make your program sound accessible, and it will be more inviting.

4. Use word-of-mouth promotion. Past participants who can heartily endorse the program are naturals to promote it to first-timers. Use both women and men to help pass the word along.

5. Make use of free radio and television advertising. Often the media provide public service announcements, enabling you to reach an entirely new group of people this way.

6. Likewise, use local and diocesan newspapers to publicize your program. Follow the short-and-sweet guidelines listed above.

7. Enlist the help of the students to write invitations to their parents for family events.

8. Combine your program with food—a surefire way to attract people. Be creative with food ideas. Food need not be fancy to be attractive.

9. Send personal invitations via snail mail or e-mail, or through personal phone calls. This takes more time but inevitably is the most effective way to promote something.

10. Believe in it! Why would you want to be there? Answering this question will give rise to some creative ideas for enthusiastic promotion.

## 10 Ways to Affirm Religious Education Teachers

1. Keep a fact sheet on every volunteer. List their birthdays, anniversaries, spouse and children's names, and anything else that might help you get to know them. Send cards when appropriate.

2. Be available before and after classes to talk with your staff. Let them know how interested you are in their experiences and with what is going on in their lives. If a problem occurs, extend your full support to your teachers. Work with the teachers to help them solve problems to everyone's satisfaction.

3. Plan special events for volunteers—a Christmas party, a spring brunch, a Mardi Gras party, a twilight retreat. Be sure to invite spouses and significant others to these events.

4. At monthly planning meetings, recognize volunteers who have gone "the extra mile" or those who are deserving of some recognition—teaching for two years, five years, ten years.

5. Show respect for the time commitment volunteers have made by making your planning sessions meaningful. Book speakers who will offer practical advice on teaching faith to youngsters.

6. Keep your teachers informed about upcoming events through a weekly or monthly newsletter.

7. Place little surprises or treats in the volunteers' boxes at special times of the year—candy on St. Nicholas Day, valentines on the class date closest to February 14, a small Lenten reflection book for their own use on Ash Wednesday. Include a note that tells the teacher, "You are doing a great job!" or "Thanks for all that you *do* for our kids here at St. Patrick's!"

8. Publicly recognize each teacher by name and grade on Catechetical Sunday. Call them to the front of the church at whatever Mass they attend. After their commitment ritual, invite the community to pray for them and then show them (through applause) how much they appreciate their participation in the religious education ministry.

9. At the end of the year, thank each catechist in an open letter in the parish bulletin. Mention something specific about each of the volunteers. For example,

"We are grateful for the countless hours Mrs. Gallagher spent organizing the seventh grade field trip to the seminary."

1 0. Give each catechist a permanent name tag on which his or her name is imprinted, along with his or her title (Fifth Grade Catechist). This not only makes your staff look more professional but makes them instantly recognizable to the children and their parents.

## 10 Tips for Faculty Development Topics

1. Workshop on how-tos for basic classroom management and organizational skills.

2. Ways to enhance teacher and student self-esteem (a lifelong process).

3. How to make Scripture come alive.

4. Using stories, poetry, music, and art to enhance the teaching moment and lesson.

5. Catholic updating, the new catechism, letters from the pope, and so on.

6. How to help children and faculty deal with the many losses in their lives.

7. Ideas that help with discipline, or what works with disruptive Johnny?

**8.** Workshop on "prayer styles," meditation, prayers of the heart, body prayer, centering.

**9.** Ideas to celebrate and make holidays and holy days more meaningful.

**10.** How to involve family in sacramental programs and family rituals in the parish and in the home.

## 10 Community Builders among Teachers

**1.** Pair up to form "birthday buddies." Send each other cards and words of encouragement on each other's birthday.

**2.** Snack and share as part of a catechist or faculty meeting. Each person brings a favorite finger food and an accompanying recipe (even if it is just "go to store and pick up bag of chips . . .").

**3.** Attend Mass together at the start and end of the school/program year.

**4.** Take turns planning short, simple prayers for faculty meetings. Do this in pairs in order to share ideas and responsibilities.

**5.** Keep a prayer-request log handy for writing down prayer needs. Read prayer needs aloud at each meeting and join in praying together for each other.

6. Invite each teacher or catechist to share one of their great ideas at a monthly faculty meeting.

7. Start a "funny board." Invite teachers to bring in favorite cartoons, quips, stories, one-liners, and other humorous pieces to share with others.

8. Have a twilight retreat, from 5:00 to 8:00 P.M., for example, and include a simple supper. Use the time to grow together spiritually.

9. Name a strength that each person brings to the group/program. Write these out on separate cards for each teacher and send out or give to that person midway through the year.

10. Form a mentoring program wherein more experienced teachers help support newer ones through a system of encouragement.

# LET US HEAR FROM YOU!

This title belongs to a series called **Resources for Religion Teachers** published by RCL.

We hope that you find it especially valuable to you as a religion teacher or parent, and that you will find the other books in the series equally informative and useful.

Please visit our website at **www.rclweb.com** for more information on this series and other RCL products or write us at:

> Resources for Christian Living
> 200 East Bethany Drive
> Allen, Texas 75002-3804

For more immediate information call our customer service line toll free at **1-877-ASK-4RCL (1-877-275-4725).**

And drop us a line to let us know what subjects you would like us to address in future selections. Your input can help us put together an even better series. Thank you.